9/29

A ROOKIE READER™

POLLY WANTS A CRACKER

By Bobbie Hamsa

Illustrations by Jerry Warshaw

Prepared under the direction of Robert Hillerich, Ph.D.

CHILDRENS PRESS ®

CHICAGO

Library of Congress Cataloging in Publication Data

Hamsa, Bobbie.
  Polly wants a cracker.

  (A Rookie Reader)
  Summary: Relates in rhyme what happens when Polly
receives all the crackers she wants.
  [1. Parrots—Fiction. 2. Stories in rhyme]
I. Warshaw, Jerry, ill. II. Title. III. Series.
PZ8.3.H189Po 1986   [E]   85-30000
ISBN 0-516-02071-4

Polly wants a cracker.

Polly got one.

Polly wants two crackers.

Polly is having fun!

Polly wants three crackers.

Polly wants four.

Polly wants five crackers.

And wants six more.

Polly wants seven crackers.

Polly wants eight.

21

Polly wants nine crackers.

23

Polly's gaining weight.

Polly wants ten crackers.
What about that?

Polly ate so many crackers,

now, Polly's fat.

WORD LIST

a	five	more	so
about	four	nine	ten
and	fun	now	that
ate	gaining	one	three
cracker	got	Polly	two
crackers	having	Polly's	wants
eight	is	seven	weight
fat	many	six	what

About the Author

Bobbie Hamsa was born and raised in Nebraska and has a Bachelor of Arts Degree in English Literature. After several years in advertising for a major firm, she and her husband, Dick Sullivan, "retired" and opened a delicatessen in Sonoma, California, where they now live with their son, John.

Bobbie Hamsa has written three other Rookie Readers; *Animal Babies*, *Dirty Larry*, and *Fast Draw Freddie*, and the Far-Fetched Pet series.

About the Artist

Jerry Warshaw, a native Chicagoan, received his training at the Art Institute of Chicago, the Chicago Academy of Fine Arts, and the Institute of Design.

Mr. Warshaw has pursued a varied free-lance career, including the illustration of the American history comic strip "The American Adventure." He served as art consultant to the Illinois Sesquicentennial Commission, and in addition to designing the official sesquicentennial emblem and flag, designed and illustrated the *Illinois Intelligencer*, the Sesquicentennial Commission's newspaper. His illustrations have appeared in numerous children's books, educational texts, magazines, and advertisements. He also designs posters, greeting cards, and sculpture.

A historian by avocation, Mr. Warshaw is a life member of the Chicago Historical Society, former president of the Civil War Round Table and the Children's Reading Round Table, and a member of the Society of Typographic Arts, the Chicago Press Club and the Art Institute of Chicago.

Mr. Warshaw lives in Evanston, Illinois, with his wife Joyce, and two cats.